# WHA SCIENTIS

A scientist is a person who wonders why. Most scientific discoveries start when a person asks a question. Why do objects fall when we drop them? How can some animals live underwater? What is beyond the stars? The answers to these questions and many more were all discovered because people wondered why.

The process of finding answers to scientific questions is called *scientific inquiry.* It involves many different steps. The first step is to make an observation. The second step is to ask a question that comes to mind as a result of making the observation. The third step is to come up with an idea that might answer your question. This idea is called a *hypothesis.* For example, after a few weeks without rain, you might observe that the plants in your garden are dying. This leads you to come up with the question, "Why are the plants dying?" Your hypothesis might be, "Plants need water to live." You would base your hypothesis on your own observations and on what you already know about the world.

The fourth step is to test your hypothesis by conducting an experiment. Just watching the plants in your garden usually does not give you enough information to find out if your hypothesis is correct. There are many other conditions besides

rainfall that might affect your plants. For example, they might be getting too much or too little sunlight. The temperature might be too hot or too cold. They could be planted in different types of soil. These factors and conditions that can change and might affect the experiment are called *variables*.

To conduct a fair experiment, you must control all of the variables except for the one you are testing. Therefore, you would need a minimum of two identical plants for such an experiment. A better experiment could be conducted with two identical sets of plants that contained five plants each. You would have to expose both sets of plants to the same amount of sunlight. You'd have to keep them at the same temperature. The only variable in your care for these plants would be in the watering. You would water one set of plants once a day for 2 weeks. You would not water the other set of plants at all.

After you completed your experiment, you would observe the results. In the example above, the plants that were not watered would die. The other plants would live. This would tell you that plants need water to live. Your idea has now been tested.

Sometimes a scientist's hypothesis turns out to be wrong. The scientist might conduct several experiments to test the hypothesis, only to discover that the results don't support it. But this does not mean the scientist has failed. The scientist still learns something by conducting the experiments and making further observations. These observations often lead to new questions, new hypotheses, new experiments, and new knowledge.

# Variables

Developed at
Lawrence Hall of Science
University of California at Berkeley

Published and Distributed by Delta Education



ISBN-10: 1-58356-844-1
ISBN-13: 978-1-58356-844-6
542-2022

7 8 9 10 11 12 QUE 13 12 11 10 09 08

# TABLE OF CONTENTS

Demonstrating that a plant needs water to live is easy. But how do scientists develop explanations for events that happen far out in space? How do they look at organisms, objects, and systems that are too small to see? How do they organize the results of their experiments?

Scientists use *instruments* to help them make observations, conduct experiments, and organize *data,* or information. Some instruments help us see things that are very tiny. These include magnifying lenses and microscopes. Other instruments show us things that are far away. These include telescopes and satellites. Instruments such as thermometers and barometers provide precise data about temperature and weather conditions. Computers help scientists to organize and analyze the data and get results much faster than any human brain can. All these instruments help scientists find answers to questions.

An important part of scientific inquiry is to make the results of experiments known to the public. Scientists write articles about their experiments and what they think they've proved. These articles are published in *scientific journals.* Some scientific journals are magazines mostly for scientists, and others are for the general public.

It is important that a scientist explain exactly how he or she conducted experiments. That allows other scientists to repeat the experiments to see if they get the same results. If they do, they will probably agree that the first scientist's ideas are correct. But sometimes other scientists do not get the same results. They may conclude that the first scientist did something wrong or that there is another explanation for the results of the original experiment. Having scientists review and ask questions about each other's work is an important step in scientific inquiry.

*Scientists gathering information in the field*

# SIR ISAAC NEWTON:
## LEARNING THROUGH EXPERIMENTING

Many people consider Sir Isaac Newton (1642–1727) to be one of the greatest scientists that ever lived. His work changed how people thought about light, gravity, and space.

Newton was born on a sheep farm 160 kilometers (100 miles) north of London. Most people did not go to school for more than a few years in those days. But Newton's teachers were very impressed with him. They encouraged his mother to send him to Cambridge, one of England's greatest universities.

After he finished his studies, Newton stayed on at Cambridge as a mathematics professor. Along with teaching, he conducted many experiments to answer questions he had about the world around him.

One of Newton's most famous discoveries was that light is made up of colors. Scientists in Newton's day were familiar with *prisms.* A prism is a clear piece of glass that breaks up light into the colors of the rainbow. But these scientists did not believe that light was actually made up of different colors. They believed that prisms changed light by making it darker. If white light became a little darker, it turned red, orange, or yellow. If it became a lot darker, the light looked green, blue, or violet.

Newton didn't believe this. He thought that the prism did not change light. It simply revealed what light was made of. His hypothesis was that sunlight was a mixture of different colors. Each of these colors was bent differently when it shone through a prism. Because the prism bent the light in different directions, the separate colors could be seen.

Newton conducted an experiment to see if he was right. He cut a small hole in a window shade hanging in his room. When the sunlight shone through the hole, it made a 5-centimeter (2-inch) image on the opposite wall. Next Newton placed a prism between the window and the wall. If all the light passing through the prism bent at the same angle, the image on the wall would be the same size. Instead the image was now over 25 centimeters (10 inches) long. And as Newton expected, the image was no longer white. It was violet at the top and red at the bottom, with a range of other colors in between.

Newton thought of a name for the colorful image he got by passing light through a prism. He called it a *spectrum*. Oddly enough, Newton's eyesight was not good. His assistant had to help him identify the rainbow of colors he created!

At first, other scientists did not believe that white light was made up of different colors. In fact, Newton spent a great deal of time defending his results to other scientists. This annoyed Newton very much. But as other scientists tried Newton's experiments, it became clear that his ideas about light were correct.

*Newton's famous experiment*

## JANE GOODALL: LEARNING THROUGH OBSERVATION

From the time she was a child, Jane Goodall (1934– ) loved animals. Born in the English countryside, she was happiest when she was outside with the horses, chickens, and other animals on the farm where she lived. Goodall read books about animals from other parts of the world. When she grew up, she wanted to study animals in the faraway land of Africa.

Goodall made her first trip to Africa in 1957, when she was 23 years old. While she was there, she met a famous scientist named Dr. Louis Leakey. Dr. Leakey was a *paleontologist*. Paleontologists study animals, plants, and people who lived millions of years ago. Leakey gave Goodall a job as his secretary. He then invited her to go on an archaeological dig in Tanzania, a country in eastern Africa.

On the trip, Dr. Leakey told Goodall about some chimpanzees in the jungles of Tanzania. He wanted someone to study these animals and observe how they behaved. He thought those observations could be used to answer questions about human behavior. Would Goodall like the job?

Goodall was thrilled at Leakey's offer. She started her observations in June 1960, in Tanzania's Gombe Stream Chimpanzee Reserve. At first, the chimps refused to come out of the trees when they saw Goodall. She had to watch them through binoculars. It was hard for her to see well through the thick leaves and branches. Although Goodall was discouraged, she did not lose her patience. After a few months, the chimpanzees began to accept her. They came out in the open and allowed her to watch them. Eventually they became very trusting. They would come right up to Goodall and allow her to groom them! It was a sign of respect and affection.

Goodall became the first human to observe how chimpanzees raise their young in the wild. She spent her days and nights in the open, watching the chimpanzees. She believed that the only way to find out how an animal really lives and behaves is to observe it in its natural environment over a long period of time.

One day, Goodall saw a chimpanzee poke a long blade of grass into a termite mound. He ate the insects that clung to the grass when he pulled it out. Later she saw some chimpanzees pulling leaves off a stick to make a termite-catching tool. This was a startling discovery. Up until then, scientists knew that many animals use tools, but they had thought only humans could create tools.

*Jane Goodall has earned the trust of chimps.*

Goodall's observations provided firsthand knowledge of chimpanzee society and behavior. She taught humans a great deal about these amazing animals. Goodall is still working with chimpanzees. She says there is so much to learn that she will never stop discovering new things about them. Jane Goodall's work shows how important observation is to scientific inquiry. By going into the wild and observing the chimpanzees in their natural habitat, she was able to learn things about them that no other scientist had known before.

## QUESTIONS TO EXPLORE

- **What are the steps involved in scientific inquiry?**
- **What is a variable?**
- **What is important to remember when you conduct a controlled experiment?**

# Toy Ducks at Sea

An accident in the Pacific Ocean led to an unusual opportunity for scientists who study ocean and wind currents. A storm struck a cargo ship sailing from Hong Kong to Tacoma, Washington, on January 10, 1992. It washed a container carrying 29,000 bathtub toys overboard south of the Aleutian Islands. Soon plastic turtles, frogs, ducks, and beavers began washing up on Alaskan beaches.

Scientists at the National Oceanic and Atmospheric Administration (NOAA) took advantage of this opportunity. A group of *oceanographers,* scientists who study the ocean, began to track the toys' journeys around the Pacific. At first, scientists followed reports from beaches where a lot of the toys washed up. Then they actively went out and searched for the toys themselves. They made charts showing where and when some toys landed. These observations gave them firsthand information about wind and ocean currents. Scientists hoped to use this information to track oil spills and discover where schools of fish travel.

The oceanographers learned some surprising things. Jim Ingraham, a scientist at NOAA, says that scientists thought it would take 4 to 6 years for the toys to make a complete circuit of the northern Pacific. Instead it took just 2.5 years. That might mean that ocean and wind currents are stronger than scientists thought. Scientists also noted that the toys traveled in a counterclockwise manner.

Even though the ducks completed their circuit of the northern Pacific, many of them are still out there. Ingraham wouldn't be surprised if some of the toys become trapped in northward-moving ice at the North Pole. These might float all the way to the Atlantic Ocean. If that happens, scientists will have a whole new ocean to explore, all thanks to a carton of shipwrecked toys!

# SWINGING THROUGH HISTORY

What do grandfather clocks have in common with children on swings? *Pendulums!*

A pendulum is a mass that hangs down from a rope, chain, or other support. When the mass is moved from its resting position and then released, the pendulum swings back and forth. The movement is called *oscillation.* Each swing takes the same length of time to complete until the pendulum runs out of energy and stops. The longer the pendulum, the fewer swings it makes in a given length of time.

Pendulums were first recognized by the Italian physicist and astronomer Galileo Galilei (1564–1642). Galileo saw a chandelier swinging from a ceiling like a pendulum. He had no way to measure how long each swing of the pendulum took. He used the rhythm of his own pulse to time the cycles. He figured out that the time it took for a pendulum to swing back and forth was always the same, no matter how far it was swinging.

Galileo thought that a pendulum could be used in timekeeping. But it was Dutch scientist Christiaan Huygens (1629–1695) who put this idea

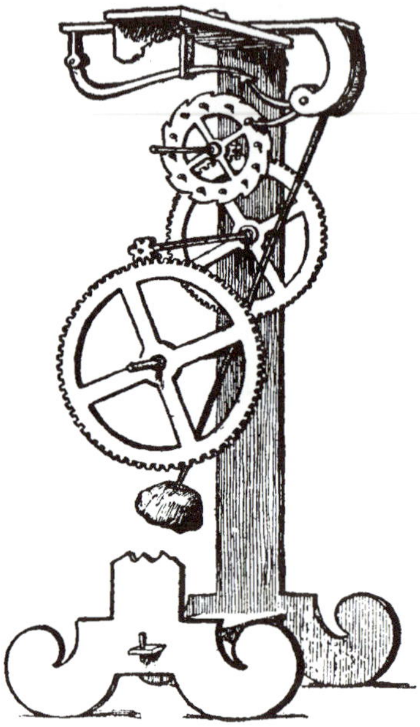

*Galileo's pendulum from 1650*

into action. Huygens was an astronomer. He needed a way to measure time as he observed the sky. Sometime around 1655, Huygens created the first reliable clock that measured seconds accurately. He used a pendulum to regulate the movement of the clock. In 1673, Huygens published a book that explained how the length of a pendulum determined the time it took to swing back and forth.

Perhaps the most common use of pendulums today is in grandfather clocks. Most of these clocks are powered by the movement of a pendulum. A grandfather clock keeps time by using a mechanism called an *escapement.* The escapement regulates the release of the mass's energy. It does this by transferring that energy to gears that move wheels on the face of the clock. As the pendulum swings back and forth, the escapement's gears move. So do the clock's hands, 1 second at a time. The only problem with this system is that the pendulum eventually runs out of energy. It moves slower, then finally stops. That is why grandfather clocks need to have their masses reset on a regular basis. More energy must be provided to the pendulum to start the process over again.

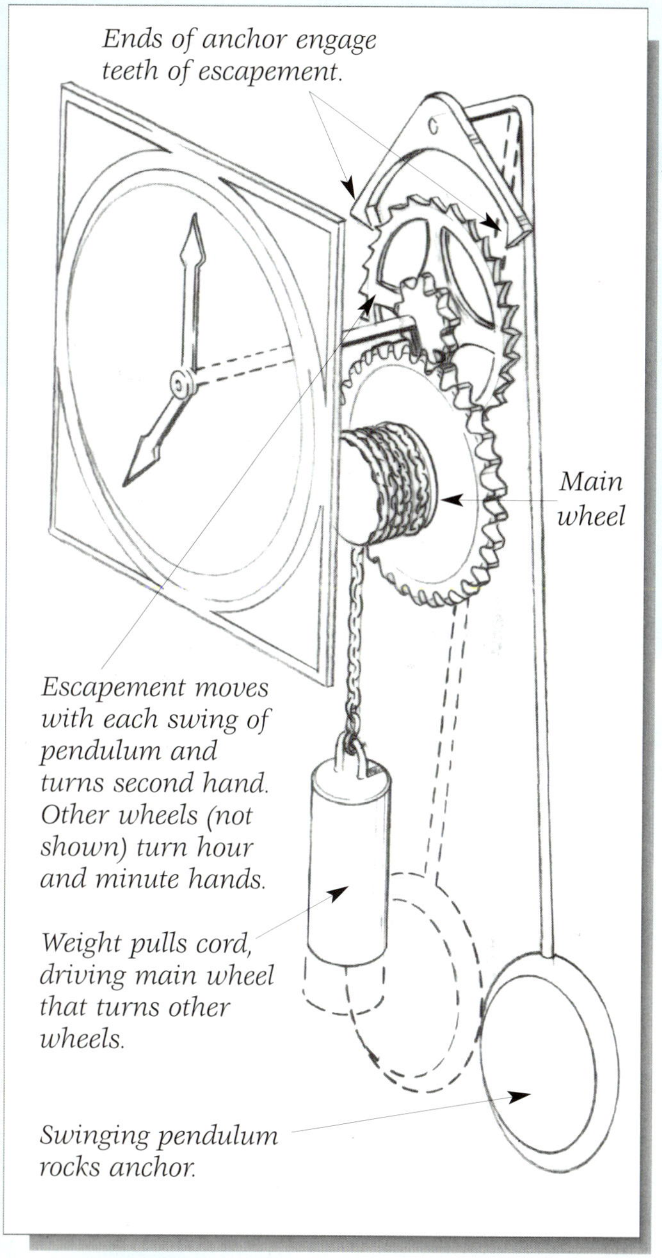


*A diagram of a grandfather clock*

You can be a pendulum, too! Next time you are on a swing, think about how your body moves through the air. You are swinging the same way a pendulum does. The energy to keep yourself moving comes from someone pushing you. The harder you are pushed, the higher and faster you swing.

# SINK OR SWIM?

Captains of boats are always on the lookout for dangers in the water. After big storms, tree trunks weighing several tons can be found floating in the sea. If a ship collides with a floating tree trunk, the ship can be damaged. Logs and other large floating objects must be avoided by ships at sea.

Some people think objects float because they are light. But a log floating at sea might have a mass of several tons. That's heavy! So why does the log float? The answer is *density*.

Think about a block of wood in the shape of a cube, 10 cm on a side. If you weigh it, you might find that the block of wood has a mass of 500 g. Now think about a block of lead exactly the same size and shape. Do you think it will weigh more or less than the block of wood? It will surely weigh more. The 10-cm cube of lead has a mass of about 11,000 g.

The two cubes are the same size, or the same *volume,* but the cube of lead is much heavier because lead is much denser than wood. There is more matter in a given volume of lead than there is in the same volume of wood. Density is all about mass per volume.

Now think about a 10-cm cube of water. If you could put the cube of water on a scale and weigh it, its mass would be 1,000 g. Compare the three cubes.

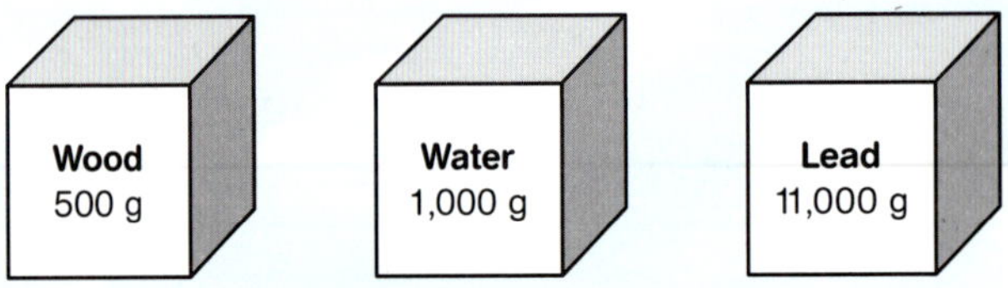


The volume of a cube can be calculated by multiplying length by width by depth. In this case, all three cubes come out to be 10 x 10 x 10 centimeters, or 1,000 cubic centimeters (cc). If density is mass per volume, we can determine the density of any object for which we know the mass and volume. Just divide the mass by the volume.

$$\textbf{Wood} = \frac{500\text{ g}}{1{,}000\text{ cc}} = 0.5\text{ g/cc} \quad \textbf{Water} = \frac{1{,}000\text{ g}}{1{,}000\text{ cc}} = 1.0\text{ g/cc} \quad \textbf{Lead} = \frac{11{,}000\text{ g}}{1{,}000\text{ cc}} = 11.0\text{ g/cc}$$

Here's one of the big ideas behind why things float or sink. If an object is less dense than water, it will float in water. If an object is denser than water, it will sink. It's that simple.

A common science activity is to make paper-cup boats out of a kind of paper that has a density of about 1.1 g/cc. Because the paper is denser than water, it should sink. But when you put a paper-cup boat into water carefully, it floats. And it will carry a load of penny "passengers," too. How is this possible?

Paper, steel, concrete, and even lead boats float because of their shapes. Boats have large air spaces inside. Air is not very dense at all. The boat should be thought of as a *system* made out of two materials, which are a dense hull and a not-very-dense volume of air inside. The end result is that a boat filled with air is a system that is much less dense than water, so it floats.

As passengers (pennies) are added to the system, the density of the system starts to change. With each added penny, the boat settles deeper into the water. Eventually the boat-air-passengers system will reach a density of 1.0, which is the density of water. (Pure water always has a density of 1.0.) One additional passenger will make the boat system denser than water, and down it goes.

What variable determines the number of passengers a boat will hold? Its volume will tell you. The bigger the boat, the more air it has included in the system. A boat can hold a lot of pennies if it contains a large volume of low-density air.

Think about this interesting experiment. Four students in Tampa, Florida, got some float-and-sink materials together. Here are what they gathered and the density of each material.

| Material | Density | Material | Density |
|---|---|---|---|
| A piece of wood | 0.5 g/cc | A piece of plastic | 1.1 g/cc |
| A piece of wax | 0.9 g/cc | A piece of rubber | 1.2 g/cc |
| A piece of ice | 0.9 g/cc | A piece of copper | 9.0 g/cc |
| A piece of tar | 1.0 g/cc | | |

What do you think the students observed when they put each material in water? Make a list of your predictions on a separate piece of paper.

The Tampa students had another idea. They made a saturated salt solution. The density of the saturated salt solution was 1.2 g/cc. They put their objects in the salt water. Do you think they got the same results, or would you expect different results? Write down your predictions and compare them with those of other students.

# SCIENCE IN THE BATHTUB

Archimedes hurried into the chamber where his friend, King Hieron, was waiting for him. "You wished to see me?" Archimedes asked.

"Yes," said King Hieron. "I need your help." The king pointed to a golden crown. "A goldsmith just delivered my new crown to me."

"It is very nice," Archimedes said, admiring the shiny crown. "Is it pure gold?"

"It's supposed to be, but I'm not sure," King Hieron replied. "I gave the goldsmith a lump of gold from which he could make the crown. The goldsmith swore that he used all of it and nothing else, but I just don't trust the man. I think he added silver to the crown and kept the leftover gold for himself. But I can't prove it. That's why I called you, Archimedes. You're the cleverest man in all of Greece. Can you prove that this crown is pure gold?"

"Of course I can," said Archimedes, although he had no idea how he would accomplish the task. "May I take the crown home to study?"

"Yes, but don't damage it and don't lose it!" King Hieron warned him.

Archimedes tucked the crown safely under his cloak. The king also gave him a piece of pure gold the same size as the one he'd given the goldsmith.

When Archimedes arrived at his home, he set the crown on a table and stared at it. "Perhaps if I weigh the crown, that will give me the answer," he mumbled to himself. He retrieved his scale and put it on the table in front of him. Then he placed the crown on one side and the lump of gold on the other. They weighed exactly the same.

"Surely the goldsmith already thought of that," Archimedes said thoughtfully. "He could have added enough silver to equal the weight of the gold. There has to be another way to solve this problem."

Archimedes thought about the king's crown for many days. He became so absorbed in the problem that he forgot to eat and he barely slept. He wandered around in a daze, his head filled with golden crowns.

"Archimedes, you are thinking too hard," said his servant one day. "Why don't you take a nice, hot bath to relax?" Archimedes nodded distractedly, and his servant hurried to fill a tub with water.

"Ahh," Archimedes sighed as he lowered himself into the bath. The hot water did feel good. But the tub was too full, and water sloshed over the sides and splashed to the floor. Archimedes stared at it.

"I'm sorry, Archimedes," said his servant. "Don't worry, I'll clean it up later."

Archimedes didn't even hear him. He just kept staring at the water. Suddenly he leaped out of the tub and ran out into the street stark naked! "Eureka!" he shouted as he ran toward King Hieron's palace. "Eureka! I have found it! I have found the answer!"

Archimedes' servant raced after him, clutching a robe. "I don't care what you've found! You can't tell King Hieron about it without wearing clothes!" the servant said.

Archimedes pulled on the robe. "Run home and bring me King Hieron's crown and the lump of gold," he told the servant. Then he rushed on toward the palace.

King Hieron was laughing when Archimedes came into the room. "I hear you've made a startling discovery!" he said. "Have you solved the problem of my crown?"

"Indeed I have," Archimedes said proudly. "I need a large jar filled to the top with water. A bowl should be placed underneath. Then I can solve this mystery for you."

King Hieron's servants hurried to get what Archimedes needed. The king leaned forward and watched eagerly as Archimedes lowered the crown into the jar of water. Some water spilled over the edge of the jar and ran into the bowl. Archimedes carefully measured the water and told the king how much was there. Then he did the same thing with the lump of gold. Everyone was startled to see that the lump of gold spilled less water than the crown.

"How can this be?" King Hieron asked. "If the crown and the gold are supposed to be the same size, wouldn't they spill the same amount of water?"

"Exactly right," Archimedes said. "This proves that the goldsmith did cheat you by adding silver to the crown. Silver is less dense than gold, so it takes a larger volume of silver to equal the mass of the gold. The goldsmith had to use more silver to make up for the gold he stole. This gave the crown a larger volume. That's why the crown spilled more water than an equal mass of pure gold."

"Archimedes, you're a genius!" King Hieron shouted, giving his friend a happy slap on the back. "Now go home and put on some proper clothes so you can be my guest at dinner tonight." The king's gaze turned hard. "Meanwhile, I have a few things to say to that goldsmith!"

# AIRPLANE BASICS

An airplane seems to defy the law of gravity. It's amazing that something so large and heavy can fly through the air! However, the reason airplanes can fly is based on solid scientific principles. Let's take a look at the whys and hows of airplane flight.

**Q:** *How can an airplane fly?*
**A:** Part of the reason an airplane flies is because air moving over and under its wings travels at different speeds. These different speeds produce lower air pressure above the wings than below them. The higher pressure under the wings pushes up. This pushing produces *lift,* one part of the force that keeps a plane in the air.

Airplane wings are not flat. The front edge of the wing is higher than the back edge. When the plane moves through the air, the bottom of the wing runs into the air, and the angle of the wing directs the air downward. The wing pushes down on the air, and the air pushes up on the wing. This produces most of the lift that keeps the airplane flying.

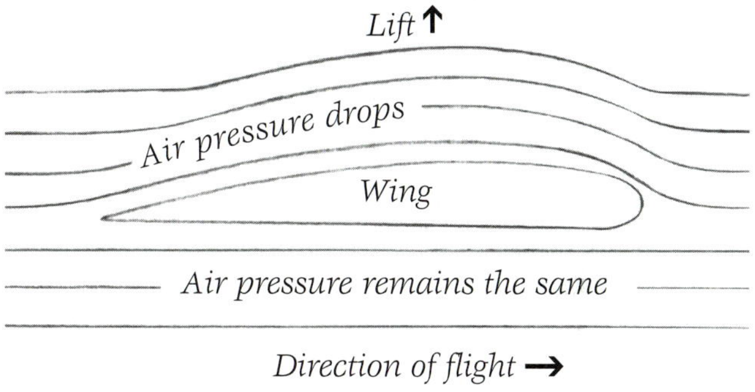


**Q:** *What other factor influences lift?*
**A:** The speed at which a plane travels is very important in determining lift. The faster the plane moves, the faster the air streams over and under the wings, and the greater the lift.

**Q:** *Planes are very heavy. How can they get up in the air?*
**A:** The lift contributed by the wings works against the weight of the plane. If the lift is greater than the weight of the plane, the plane will rise into the air.

**Q:** *Is a plane ever too heavy to fly?*
**A:** Yes. Designers carefully figure out how much weight a plane can carry and still have enough lift to stay in the air.

**Q:** *How does a pilot make a plane rise and fall in the air?*
**A:** If a pilot wants the plane to rise, he or she will increase the tilt of the wings while keeping the speed of the plane the same. To lower the plane, he or she will decrease the tilt. A plane will also rise if its speed is increased, and it will fall if its speed is decreased.

**Q:** *How do pilots change the tilt of the wings?*
**A:** Devices called *flaps* extend out from the edges of the wings. These flaps are usually tucked into the wings during level flight. If extra lift is needed, the pilot extends the flaps out and down along the back edges of the wings.

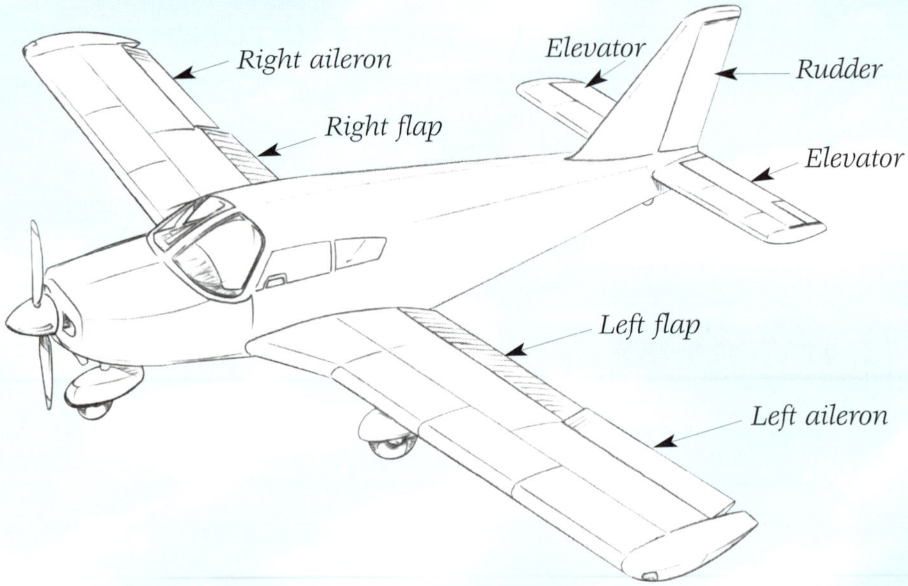


**Q:** *What is* drag?
**A:** Drag is the resistance of air to objects moving through it. This slows down the plane.

**Q:** *How are planes designed to overcome drag?*
**A:** Planes are *streamlined,* or designed so that air flows over them smoothly. Slots can also be placed in the wings so that air flows through the wings rather than building up in front of them and slowing the plane down.

**Q:** *How do planes move and turn in the air?*
**A:** Pilots use three control devices to fly a plane. These are *elevators, rudders,* and *ailerons.* Elevators are located on the tail. When the pilot pulls backward on the *yoke* in the cockpit, the

elevators move up. This lowers the tail and lifts the plane. Moving the yoke forward lowers the elevators and sends the plane into a dive. The rudder is also located on the tail. It is operated by pedals in the cockpit. The rudder allows the plane to turn. When the right rudder pedal is pressed, the rudder turns the plane to the right. Ailerons are located far out on the wings and are operated from the yoke. Turning the yoke to the left raises the left aileron and lowers the right aileron. This forces the plane to bank to the left. Instruments in the cockpit tell the pilot what direction the plane is moving, what its altitude is, and other important facts.

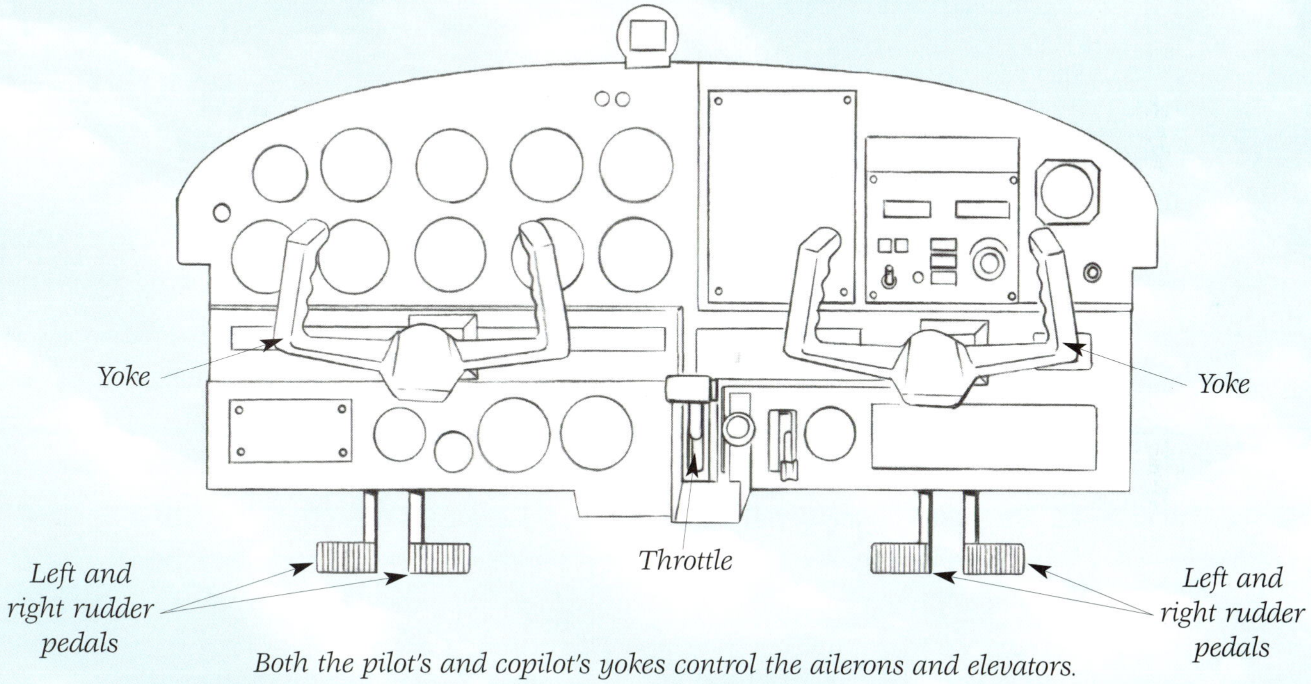


*Both the pilot's and copilot's yokes control the ailerons and elevators. Their pedals operate the rudder. The throttle controls engine power and speed.*

## QUESTIONS TO EXPLORE

- **What gives an airplane most of its lift?**
- **What other factors help keep an airplane in the air?**
- **What factors need to be considered when designing an airplane?**

# EXPERIMENTAL DESIGNS

There are very few similarities between a plane from 1903 and one from today. Airplane designs have changed dramatically over the past 100 years!

A plane from the early 1900s may look funny and primitive to us, but it was a great advance over what had come before. People had been trying to fly for thousands of years. Early designs consisted of giant wings made of cloth that were strapped onto a person's arms. But these designs never worked. A person's arm and chest muscles simply aren't strong enough to lift him or her off the ground. It wasn't until the invention of motorized engines that airplane flight became possible.

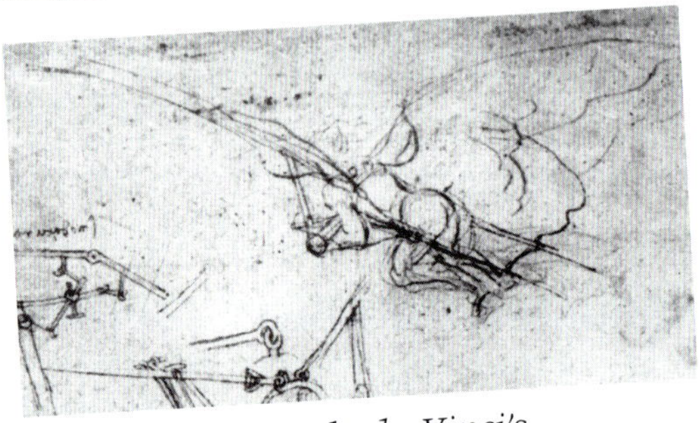

*Leonardo da Vinci's flying machine from 1490*

Orville and Wilbur Wright, two brothers from Dayton, Ohio, had long been fascinated with the idea of flight. They built and flew gliders and designed their own small engine. On December 17, 1903, on a beach in Kitty Hawk, North Carolina, Orville Wright made the first airplane flight. It was a 12-second, 36-meter (120-foot) journey into history. The Wright *Flyer* had two propellers which pulled the plane through the air. These were powered by a 16-horsepower, gasoline engine. The *Flyer* was a *biplane,* meaning it had two sets of wings. These 12-meter (40-foot) wings were made of a wooden framework covered with fabric. Cross wires kept the structure rigid.

*The Wright brothers making their first airplane flight in 1903*

Biplanes and other multiwinged craft were favored during the early days of airplane design. The many wings on these types of airplanes provided superior lift. But they also produced greater drag, since the planes had more surface area to move through the air. Later *cantilever* wings were developed. Cantilever wings are supported only at one end (the end attached to the plane). They get their strength from structural supports inside the wings. Cantilever wings led to the development of the *monoplane,* a plane with a single set of wings. By the 1930s, the monoplane was the most popular airplane design.

Early planes were powered by propellers, but these planes could not move very fast. The invention of the jet engine allowed planes to fly much faster. In a jet engine, powerful *turbines,* or fans, push air into the engine. There it is compressed and sprayed with fuel in a heat-resistant chamber. The air catches fire, and burning gases rush out of a combustion chamber with great force. This provides the energy to move the plane. The first jet engine was designed in 1937 by British pilot and engineer Frank Whittle. A German designer named Hans von Ohain used Whittle's idea to create a jet engine. In 1939, the German *Heinkel He-178* became the first jet-powered aircraft to take to the sky.

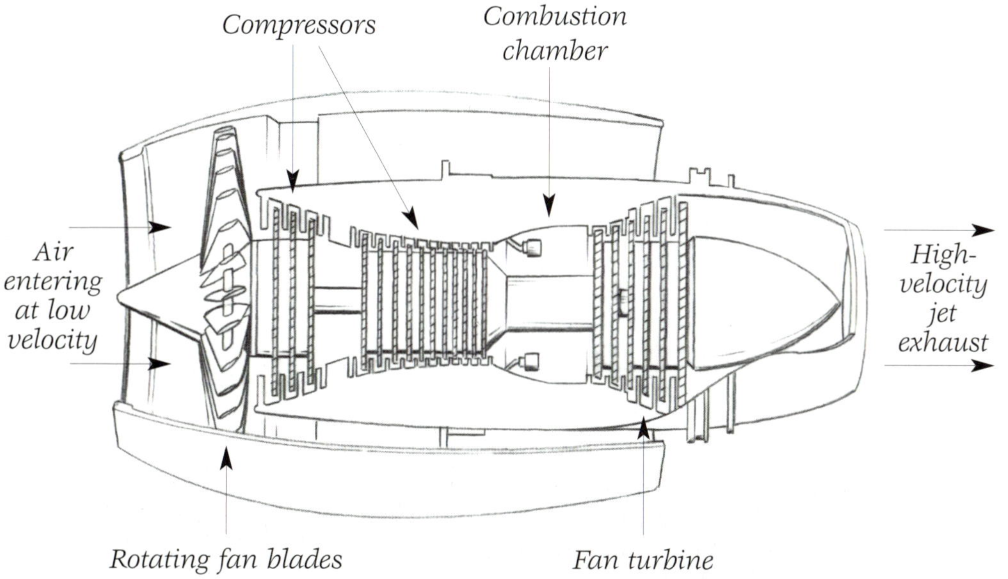


*A diagram of a jet engine*

The first American-built jet airplane was the *Bell XP-59*. It was made in 1942 using a General Electric I-16 turbojet adapted from Whittle's design. The first jet engine of exclusively American design was produced by the Westinghouse Electric Corporation for the U.S. Navy in 1944.

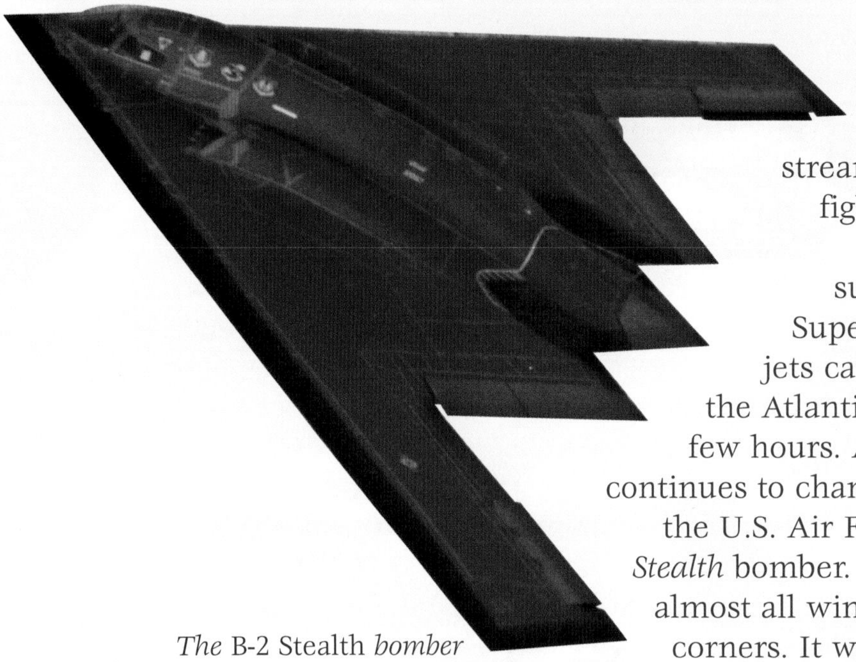
*The* B-2 Stealth *bomber*

As time passed, planes became larger, faster, and more streamlined. Today jet fighters used by the military fly at supersonic speeds. Supersonic passenger jets carry people across the Atlantic Ocean in just a few hours. And plane design continues to change. In July 1989, the U.S. Air Force flew the *B-2 Stealth* bomber. This flat plane is almost all wing and has angled corners. It was designed to be almost invisible to radar.

The way planes are designed has changed over the years, too. Early planes were one-of-a-kind, hand-built out of wood, wire, and fabric. The only way to test them was by flying them. Later planes were tested in huge buildings called *wind tunnels*. Here designers could see how air would flow over them and affect their ability to fly. Today planes are made entirely out of metal. They are packed with more than 1 million parts controlled by sophisticated computer systems. In the 1990s, Boeing created the 777 passenger jet. It was the first plane to be designed and tested completely by computers. We've certainly come a long way from a simple airplane lifting off for its 12-second journey over a North Carolina beach!

*The Boeing 777 passenger jet*

# GREAT NAMES IN AVIATION HISTORY

*Aviation* is the science of building and flying heavier-than-air craft, including airplanes, gliders, and helicopters. Many people have worked hard to make new discoveries in aviation. Some of them, such as the Wright brothers, designed and built airplanes and other flying machines. Others, such as Bessie Coleman and Chuck Yeager, were pilots who broke new ground with their brave adventures. And like William Boeing, some took a love of flying, turned it into a business, and developed amazing new advances in aviation.

*The Wright brothers, Wilbur (left) and Orville (right), and their sister Katherine*

# ORVILLE AND WILBUR WRIGHT:

## THE FIRST TO FLY

Orville Wright (1871–1948) and Wilbur Wright (1867–1912) were two brothers who ran a bicycle shop in Dayton, Ohio. They liked to tinker with machines. On December 17, 1903, they made the first heavier-than-air flight. Ten years later, in 1913, Orville wrote this account of that first flight.

During the night of December 16th a strong cold wind blew from the north. When we arose on the morning of the seventeenth, the puddles of water, which had been standing about the camp since the recent rains, were covered with ice. The wind had a velocity of 10 to 12 metres per second (22 to 27 miles an hour). We thought it would die down before long, and so remained indoors the early part of the morning. But when ten o'clock arrived, and the wind was as brisk as ever, we decided that we had better get the machine out and attempt a flight. We hung out the signal for the men of the Life-saving Station. We thought that by facing the flyer into a strong wind, there ought to be no trouble in launching it from the level ground about camp. We realized the difficulties of flying in so high a wind, but estimated that the added dangers in flight would be partly compensated for by the slower speed in landing....

We had a 'Richard' hand anemometer with which we measured the velocity of the wind. Measurements made just before starting the first flight showed velocities of 11 to 12 metres per second, or 24 to 27 miles per hour. Measurements made just before the last flight

gave between 9 and 10 metres per second. One made just afterwards showed a little over 8 metres. The record of the Government Weather Bureau at Kitty Hawk gave the velocity of the wind between the hours of ten-thirty and twelve o'clock, the time during which the four flights were made, as averaging 27 miles at the time of the first flight and 24 miles at the time of the last.

With all the knowledge and skill acquired in thousands of flights in the last ten years, I would hardly think today of making my first flight on a strange machine in a 27-mile wind, even if I knew that the machine had already been flown and was safe. After these years of experience, I look with amazement upon our audacity in attempting flights with a new and untried machine under such circumstances. Yet faith in our calculations and the design of the first machine, based upon our tables of air pressure, obtained by months of careful laboratory work, and confidence in our system of control developed by three years of actual experiences in balancing gliders in the air had convinced us that the machine was capable of lifting and maintaining itself in the air, and that, with a little practice, it could be safely flown.

# BESSIE COLEMAN:
## BREAKING BARRIERS

By 1920, airplanes were beginning to appear in the sky regularly. Pilots from World War I (1914–1918) flew their little planes from one community to another, performing *barnstorming* shows. They performed daring aerial acrobatics and took people for quick rides. But nearly all these pilots were white men. Flying was considered too dangerous for women, especially black women. Bessie Coleman (1893–1926) changed all of that.

Coleman came from a poor family in Waxahatchie, Texas. Her mother was African American and her father was Native American. After her father left the family, Coleman was forced to quit school. She had to watch her younger sisters while her mother went out to work.

Coleman knew that education was the only way to make her life better than her mother's. She wanted to escape poverty. So she was thrilled at the chance to go back to school when her sisters were older. She studied for a year at the all-black Langston Industrial College in Langston, Oklahoma. She had to leave college when her money ran out. Then she moved to Chicago, Illinois, to live with her brother. Jobs were easier to find in the northern cities. The more industrialized northern economy demanded a lot of workers for its factories. There was also less prejudice against blacks in the northern cities, which made it easier for them to find jobs. Coleman was soon working as a manicurist in a barber shop.

Coleman read newspaper articles about the Wright brothers and other early pilots. She was surprised to learn that some of these pilots were women. She became fascinated with the idea of flying. Coleman vowed that someday, somehow, she would learn to fly a plane.

Working in the barber shop, Coleman became friendly with Robert Abbott. He was the editor of Chicago's African American newspaper, the *Defender.* The *Defender* wrote about Eugene Bullard, a black pilot who had flown with the French air service in World War I. When she saw this, Coleman told Abbott she wanted to fly, too. Abbott did some research. He found that no American flying schools would accept a black female student. He recommended that Coleman go to France to study. Racial attitudes were much more open there than they were in the U.S.

In 1920, Coleman left for France. She was accepted by the best flying school in France. On June 15, 1921, she became the first black woman to earn a pilot's license.

Coleman returned to the United States. She gave speeches and performed in air shows all over the country. It was her dream to start her own flying school, one that would accept blacks and women. Sadly Coleman was killed in a plane crash in Jacksonville, Florida, on April 30, 1926. She died before she had enough money to open her school.

Despite her early death, Coleman inspired other aviators to fulfill her dream. In 1929, William Powell, a young black pilot, opened the Bessie Coleman Aero Club in Los Angeles, California. Then anyone could learn to fly, regardless of color or gender. Bessie Coleman's dream finally came true.

## CHUCK YEAGER:
## FASTER THAN THE SPEED OF SOUND

On October 14, 1947, people at Muroc Air Base in the California desert heard a sound no one had ever heard before. A sonic boom echoed over the base. For the first time in history, a plane had flown at *Mach 1,* the speed of sound. The pilot of that plane was Chuck Yeager (1923– ).

The speed of sound is 1,055 kilometers per hour (660 miles per hour) above 13,500 meters (45,000 feet). Pilots had noticed that as their speeds approached the speed of sound, their planes began to shake violently. Usually they could not control them. Some planes were even ripped apart by these terrible forces, and several pilots were killed. Scientists figured out that the forces battering these planes were *shock waves.* As a plane flies, it causes waves of air pressure to move in front of it. If a slow-flying plane is behind these waves, it is not affected by them. But as a plane approaches the speed of sound, it catches up to its own shock waves. These waves surround the plane and expose it to tremendous stress.

Breaking the sound barrier was the only way people could ever fly into space. But many doubted it could be done. They were sure any plane that flew that fast would be destroyed by the shock waves. Some people even thought the sound barrier was a physical wall into which the plane would crash.

Chuck Yeager didn't believe any of this. Neither did a group of scientists at Bell Aircraft Corporation. They worked with the U.S. Air Force to design an experimental plane to fly faster than the speed of sound. The test pilot for this plane, called the *X-1,* was Chuck Yeager.

Yeager was born in West Virginia in 1923. By the time he finished high school, the United States had entered World War II (1939–1945). Yeager joined the Army Air Corps (now the Air Force) and was sent to England. He flew several bombing missions to Germany and shot down enemy planes. On one of these trips, Yeager himself was shot down behind enemy lines in France. With the help of French citizens, he managed to avoid capture and escaped back to England.

After the war, Yeager worked as a test pilot at Wright Field in Dayton, Ohio (now Wright Patterson Air Base). Wright Field was a center for testing new planes. Yeager soon won a reputation as a daring, confident pilot. It was his cool-headedness and self-assured attitude that led to his being picked as the test pilot for the *X-1.* That flight has been called "the greatest since the first successful flight of the original Wright brothers' airplane."

After his record-setting flight, Yeager broke the sound barrier many more times. In one flight, he flew at *Mach 2.5,* two and a half times the speed of sound. Later Yeager flew combat missions during the Vietnam War (1955–1975). He also helped train the astronauts who would launch America into space and onto the Moon.

## WILLIAM BOEING: AVIATION PIONEER

The aircraft industry didn't even exist when William Boeing (1881–1956) left Yale University in 1903. He wanted to make his fortune in the Northwest timber industry. The Detroit-born engineering student was very successful. By 1908, he had moved to Seattle, Washington, a rich man.

Boeing had a great interest in aviation. In 1910, he went to Los Angeles to attend the first American air meet. While there, Boeing tried to get a ride in one of the airplanes. But none of the pilots would take him up. When Boeing returned to Seattle, he was disappointed at his failure to get up in the air. He was also determined to learn more about the new science of aviation.

For the next 5 years, Boeing met regularly with George Conrad Westervelt. Westervelt was a Navy engineer who had taken several aeronautics courses at the Massachusetts Institute of Technology (MIT). Together the men checked out several biplanes. They actually got to ride in an early biplane that required the pilot and passenger to sit out on the wings! Westervelt later wrote that he "could never find any definite answer as to why it held together." Both he and Boeing were convinced they could build a better biplane.

In 1915, Boeing returned to California to take flying lessons. While he was away, Westervelt designed a seaplane in Boeing's boathouse. The men combined their initials to name the plane the *B & W.* Unfortunately the Navy assigned Westervelt to a post in the eastern U.S. before the plane was finished. Boeing went on to finish the plane in 1916. When it was time for the *B & W*'s first flight, the pilot was late. Boeing became so impatient that he climbed into the cockpit and took the plane up himself!

On July 15, 1916, Boeing incorporated his airplane manufacturing business as Pacific Aero Products Company. A year later, he changed the name to the Boeing Airplane Company. He hired top engineers to design new planes. He also built a wind tunnel at the University of Washington so the school could offer courses in aeronautics.

Boeing's company grew when the Navy bought some of his planes for use in World War I. But after the war, there was no military market for airplanes. To keep his company alive, Boeing built furniture and boats. Meanwhile, Boeing designed several commercial biplanes.

In 1923, Boeing built the *Model 40A* mail plane. Four years later, in 1927, a *Model 40A* featuring a lighter, air-cooled engine won a contract from the U.S. Postal Service. During the first year, Boeing's company carried 376,745 kilograms (837,211 pounds) of mail and 1,863 passengers.

By the late 1920s, biplanes were becoming outdated. In 1930, Boeing's company unveiled its first monoplane. Called the *Monomail,* the plane was the most revolutionary commercial airplane of its time. It was all metal, with a sleek, low-wing design.

In 1934, the United States government passed laws that made it illegal for airplane manufacturers to also own airlines. Because of these new laws, Boeing was split into three separate companies. These were United Air Lines, United Aircraft, and the Boeing Airplane Company. Boeing was so disgusted by this government interference that he resigned as chairman of the company. He left aviation to raise horses.

Despite William Boeing's departure, his company continued to grow. The Boeing Company went on to produce the first pressurized airliner. It has produced World War II bombers and passenger jets. Boeing has also made Air Force One (used by the president of the United States), the lunar orbiter used in the Apollo Moon landings, and the space shuttle. Today Boeing is the largest aerospace company in the world. It is a leader in commercial, defense, and space flight. It's been a long time since the company's founder was refused an airplane flight back in 1910!

## QUESTIONS TO EXPLORE

- **Which famous aviator broke the sound barrier?**
- **What were some of the problems Bessie Coleman had to overcome to be a pilot?**
- **What do all of these famous people have in common?**

# BUILD YOUR OWN PAPER AIRPLANE

You can investigate airplane design by building your own paper airplanes. These paper planes will serve as models of real airplanes. They will help you conduct controlled experiments to find out how changing the design of a plane affects its ability to fly.

## Broad-Wing Flyer

**1.** Start with a standard sheet of paper. Fold one corner down and across. Line the corner up with the edge of the sheet and crease the paper (a). Then fold the upper point down and across (b).

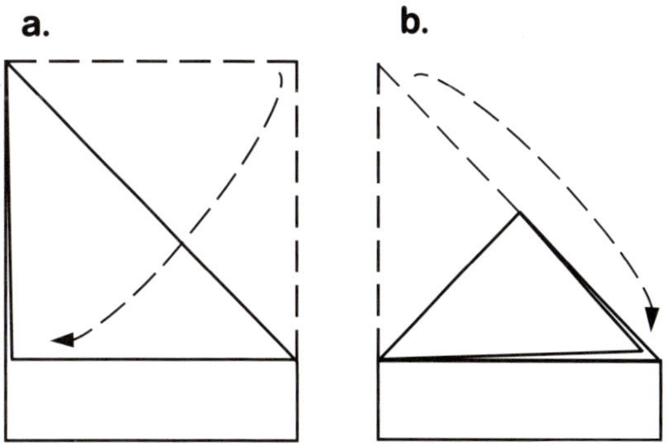


**2.** Fold the sheet in half (c) to create a center line (d). Fold the point down to the line formed by the edge of the paper (e).

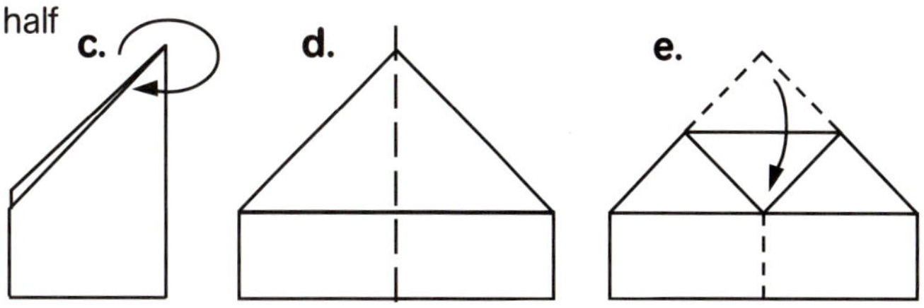


**3.** Fold the plane in half with the points and folds inside (f). Fold the wings down on the dotted line (g), first on one side (h), then on the other (i).

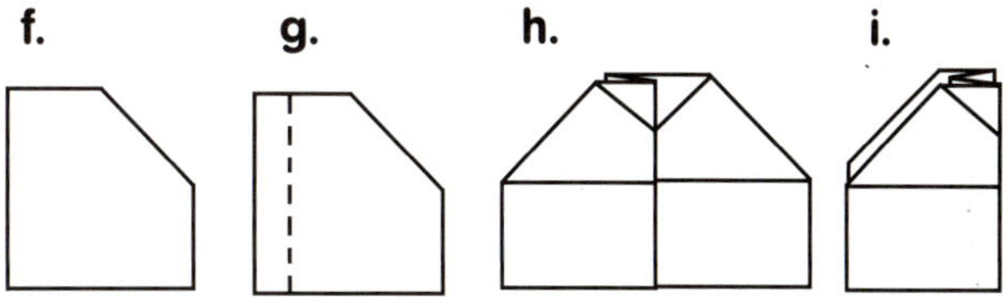


**4.** Finish the plane. Tape the front edges of the wings and the nose closed. Fold the tips of the wings up for stability. Cut some flaps in the back edges of the wings. Adjust the flaps for control.

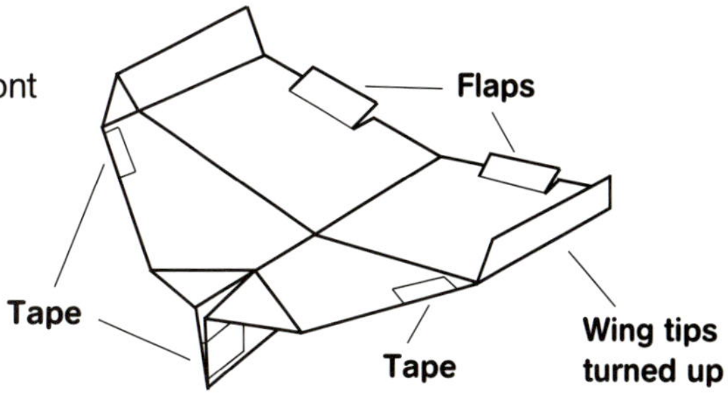

# Narrow-Wing Flyer

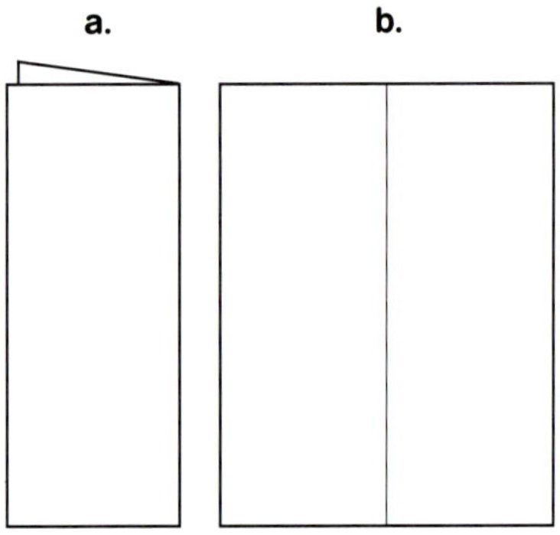


**1.** Fold a standard sheet of paper in half (a) to establish a center line (b).

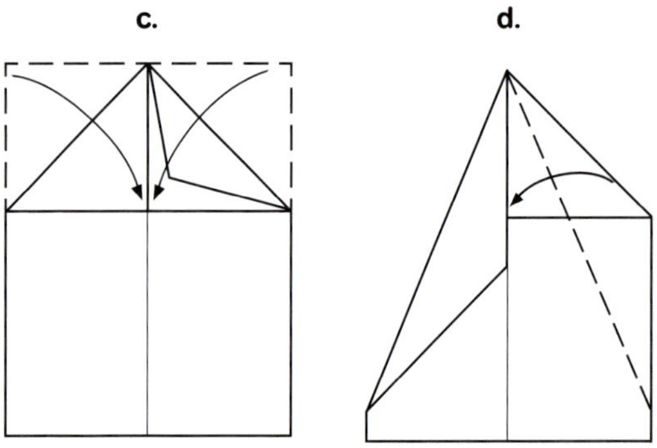


**2.** Fold the top two corners down to the center line (c). Fold the two sides to the center line using the dotted line as a guide (d).

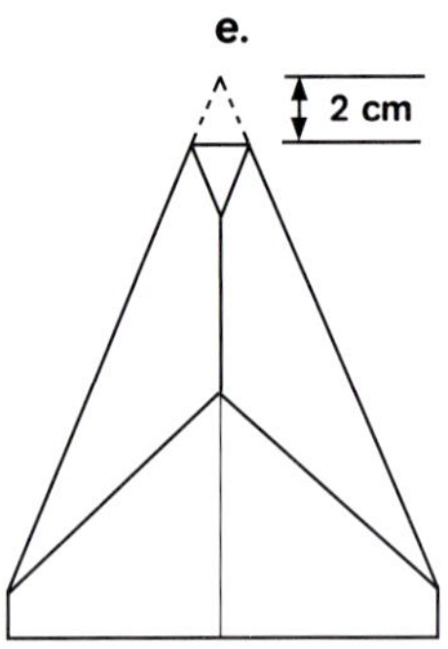


**3.** Fold the pointed tip down 2 cm (0.8 in.). Crease it firmly (e).

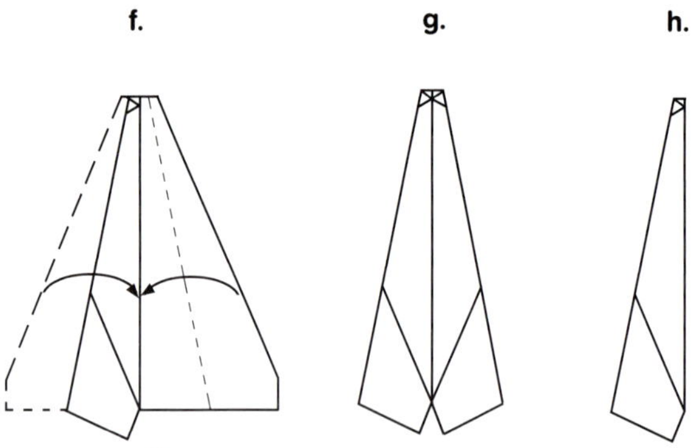


**4.** Turn the airplane over. Fold the sides to the center line one more time (f, g). Fold the plane back on the center line (h).

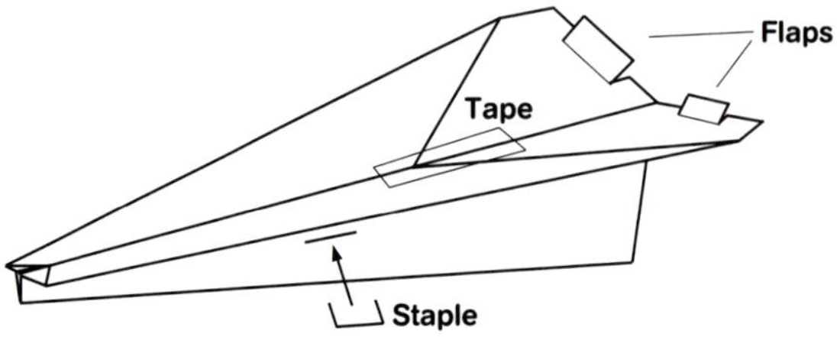


**5.** Finish the plane. Reach into the folds and grip the center-line fold. This is the plane's body. Arrange the wings and staple the body, or put a piece of tape across the wings as indicated. Cut some flaps to fine-tune the flight of the plane.

Now that you have made your planes, give them each a test flight! Which plane flies farther? Which one stays in the air longer? Experiment by changing the planes' designs. For example, you might fold up the tips of the wings. Or try bending the tail flaps downward. How do these design changes affect the flight of each plane? How could you change the designs so that the planes fly straighter or curve in the air?

## Another Fun Flyer

Make this flyer according to the diagram below. Give it a test flight, and see what happens. Think about all the different variables you could change that might affect the outcome of the flight.

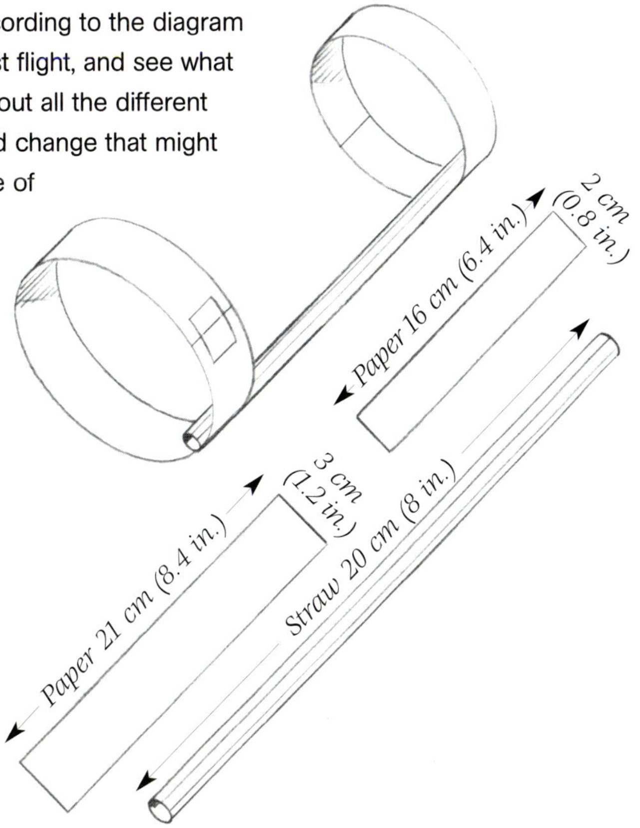


## Things to Think About

Conduct tests to answer these questions about the design of your flyer. After you've collected your data, create a graph that shows the test results.

**1)** What happens when you change the number of loops on the flyer?

**2)** What happens when you change the positions of the loops?

**3)** What happens when you change the length of the straw?

# FLINGERS

Thousands of years ago, warriors created slingshots to attack their enemies. Hundreds of years ago, attacking armies used machines called *catapults* to hurl stones and other heavy objects at the walls of castles. Today high-tech catapults fling fighter jets from the decks of ships. All of these devices harness energy and use it to propel objects into the air with great force.

In medieval times, small catapults were used to throw javelins, darts, and small rocks. Catapults allowed objects to travel farther and faster than if they were simply thrown by human arms. Larger catapults were mounted on wooden platforms. Ropes were used to pull back the propelling mechanism. These ropes were wound onto a winch as the mechanism was pulled back and loaded with a heavy stone. When the ropes were let go, the force was great enough to throw the heavy object high and far. One type of catapult, called a *ballista,* could throw stones weighing up to 45 kilograms (100 pounds).

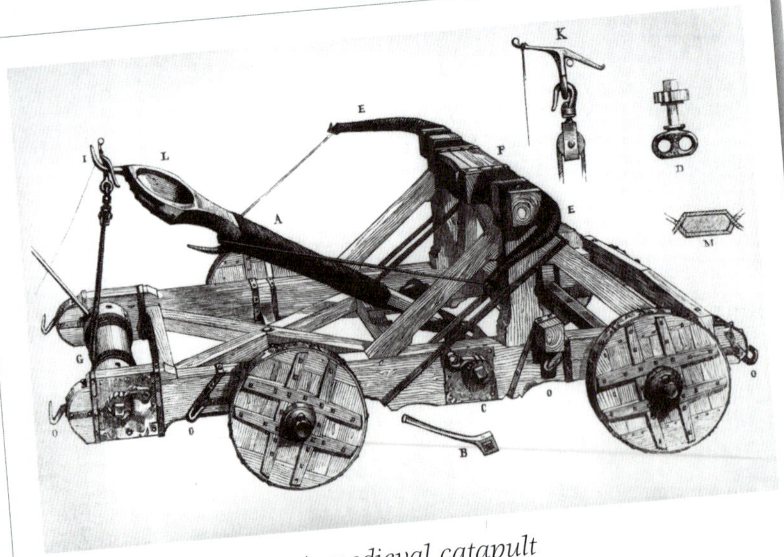

*A medieval catapult*

During World Wars I (1914–1918) and II (1939–1945), catapults were used to drop *depth charges* deep underwater. These were containers filled with explosives used to destroy enemy submarines. The catapults were mounted on the sterns of ships. A depth charge did not have to strike a direct hit on a submarine to destroy it. The impact of the exploding bomb was usually enough to severely damage any nearby submarine. Catapults allowed the depth charges to be released in a broader area around a ship.

*A jet taking off from the deck of an aircraft carrier*

Today fighter jets take off at high speed from the decks of huge ships called *aircraft carriers*. These planes need to travel very fast to get into the air. Carrier decks aren't long enough to allow a plane to get up the necessary speed. So the plane is hooked into a catapult. The catapult uses explosives or *hydraulics* to create enough force to propel the plane off the deck.

Catapults aren't only used for warfare. They are also used for sports and acrobatics. Circus acrobats use boards similar to seesaws to launch each other up into the air. Gymnasts jump off springboards to gain enough height for vaults. Athletes use fiberglass poles as catapults to push themselves over a bar in the track and field event of pole vaulting. Think about the way a ball is flung from a lacrosse stick or out of a pitcher's hand. These are catapults, too!

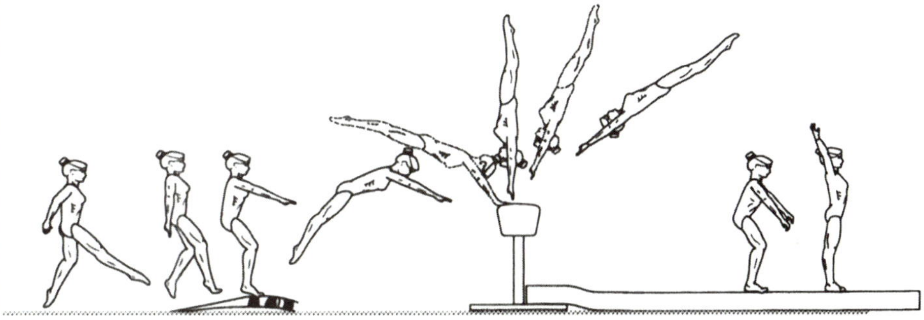

*A diagram of a gymnast vaulting off a springboard*

# PROVE IT!

"I can't believe it!" Tyrell moaned. "I've just got to have a pair of those new Super Pro 2000 sneakers. But they cost over a hundred dollars!"

"What do you need such an expensive pair of shoes for?" his friend Ryan asked. He tossed a basketball toward a hoop at the community center. "I'll bet those Super Pros aren't any better than these 40-dollar Panthers I'm wearing."

"For a hundred dollars, they've *got* to be better," Tyrell insisted as he grabbed the rebound. "They've got a special pump that makes you jump higher and run faster. At least that's what their TV commercial says. And my favorite basketball player wears them!"

"Listen up!" yelled a voice from the sideline. The boys turned and saw Lisa Monroe, one of the community center coaches. "If you want to find the best pair of sneakers, I've got an idea for you."

Tyrell and Ryan hurried to hear what Lisa had to say. Their friends, Hua and Edgar, came over, too.

Lisa held up a letter. "The *Daily Journal* is working on an article about the best sneakers for kids. They asked the community center to get some boys and girls together to test different brands and tell them which sneakers are best. Are you interested?"

"You bet!" Tyrell said. Everyone else agreed.

"Okay. Meet me here at ten o'clock on Saturday morning, and we'll get to work."

Tyrell was the first one to arrive at the basketball court on Saturday. Ryan, Edgar, and Hua showed up soon after. Lisa was the last to arrive. She had two people from the newspaper with her. One was a writer named John Hanson, and the other was a photographer named Sue Mendez. All the adults were carrying shoe boxes.

"Here's how our test will work," John explained as he spread the boxes out over the floor. "We've got six different brands of sneakers here. Each of you will put on a pair. Then you'll run down the length of the court as fast as you can. Next you'll shoot a few baskets and do some quick moves around the court. When you're done, you'll fill out a chart to describe how the sneakers feel. We want to know which ones you like best. Which ones help you run faster, jump higher, and move better?"

"Have you got any Super Pro 2000s in there?" Tyrell asked, peeking at the boxes.

"Yes, but I'm not going to tell you which ones they are," John said with a grin. "If you know what brand you're wearing, that might influence your decision. That's why none of these boxes have logos on them. We've also stripped off any identifying marks on the sneakers. We want you to make your decisions based on the sneakers themselves, not what you've heard on TV. Are you ready to get started?"

"You bet!" Tyrell said. Lisa pulled pairs of sneakers out of numbered boxes, while John made notes about who had which pair. Then all the kids lined up to race down the court.

Tyrell didn't like the first pair of sneakers he tried. They were heavy and made his feet drag. He came in last in the race, and his feet felt tired after just a few jumps at the basket.

The second pair Tyrell tried was very comfortable, but they were slippery. He almost fell trying to dodge around Hua on the court. She easily stole the ball from him and floated up to the basket.

Tyrell and his friends ran and jumped all morning. In between, they flopped down on the sidelines and filled in charts about the shoes. They gave each pair of sneakers a numerical rating. The rating was based on how comfortable they were and how easy it was to move around in them. Tyrell gave his first pair of shoes a two out of ten, because he didn't like them very much. The last pair he tried was the best, and he gave them an eight. Meanwhile, the photographer moved around the court with the kids, her camera snapping and flashing.

"Okay!" Lisa said when everyone had tried every pair of shoes. She and John studied the charts and compared notes. "Here are the results. The shoes that came in first were the Fiery Flyers. They had an average score of seven and a half. The worst shoes were the Super Pro 2000s. They only scored an average of four."

"No way!" Tyrell called out. "Everyone knows that Super Pros are the best. I bet I gave them a high score."

Lisa checked her notes. "Tyrell, you gave them a two and said they felt like lead weights around your ankles." Everyone laughed.

John asked each of the kids how they felt about the results. Then he told them to be sure to get a copy of Monday's paper, because they would all be in it.

On Monday morning, Tyrell raced down to breakfast and grabbed the paper off the kitchen table. Sure enough, there he was, running down the basketball court. He scanned the article until he found his name and read the words he had said to John Hanson on Saturday. "I never realized how much TV influences what people want to buy," he'd said. "I learned that just because something costs a lot and has lots of special features, it's not necessarily the best product. It's what's in the sneakers that counts!"

# GLOSSARY

**Aeronautics** The science dealing with the operation of aircraft.

**Aileron** A movable airfoil at the trailing edge of an airplane wing that controls the banking of the airplane.

**Anemometer** An instrument used to measure the speed of wind.

**Astronomer** A scientist who studies objects and events in the solar system and beyond.

**Bank** To tilt sideways when turning.

**Barometer** An instrument used to measure the pressure of the atmosphere, which assists in forecasting the weather.

**Circuit** A course around something, such as the circular path in which an ocean current might flow.

**Combustion chamber** A closed space where something burns, often explosively, such as gasoline in a motor.

**Density** The ratio of the mass of a material in proportion to its volume.

**Elevator** A movable airfoil attached to the tail of a plane that controls motion up and down.

**Glider** An aircraft that has wings but no engine.

**Hydraulics** Operation by the pressure of water or other liquids in motion.

**Hypothesis** A proposed answer to a question.

**Lacrosse** A ballgame where players use long-handled nets to catch and throw the ball and score goals.

**Oceanographer** A scientist who studies the ocean.

**Paleontologist** A scientist who studies what life was like millions of years ago.

**Pendulum** A mass hung from a fixed point, free to swing back and forth when put in motion.

**Pressurized** Maintaining a pressure higher than the surroundings.

**Prism** A piece of transparent material that separates light into a spectrum.

**Rudder** A movable airfoil attached to the rear of an airplane that controls the direction of flight on a horizontal plane.

**Spectrum** The name for the colorful rainbow seen when a beam of light passes through a prism.

**Supersonic** Traveling faster than the speed of sound.

**System** A set of objects that are related in some way and can be isolated for study.

**Theory** A set of principles that explains a natural event.

**Velocity** The rate at which an object moves in a certain direction.

**Winch** A machine that has a roller on which a rope is wound.